About the Series

In 1881, Sherlock Holmes, while working in the chemical laboratory of St Bartholomew's hospital in London, met Dr John Watson, an army surgeon recently returned to England. Watson was looking for lodgings. Holmes had just found some which were too large for his needs and wanted someone to share the rent. So it was that Holmes and Watson moved into 221B Baker Street. It was the beginning of a partnership which was to last more than twenty years and one which would make 221B Baker Street one of the most famous addresses in all of England.

Some credit for that partnership must also go to Mrs Hudson, Sherlock Holmes' landlady and housekeeper. It was she who put up with a lodger who made awful smells with his chemical experiments, who played the violin at any time of the day or night, who kept cigars in the coal scuttle, and who pinned his letters to the wooden mantelpiece with the blade of a knife!

So it is perhaps not unfitting that the only original documents which are known to have survived from those twenty years are now owned by Mrs Susan Stacey, a grandniece of that same Mrs Hudson. They include three of Dr Watson's notebooks or, more accurately, two notebooks and a diary which has been used as a notebook. The rest is an odd assortment, from letters and newspaper clippings to photographs and picture postcards. The whole collection has never been seen as anything more than a curiosity. The notebooks do not contain any complete accounts of cases – only jottings – though some of these were very probably made on the spot in the course of actual investigations. Occasionally, something has been pinned or pasted to a page of a notebook. There are some rough sketches and, perhaps the most interesting, there are many ideas and questions which Watson must have noted down so that he could discuss them with Holmes at some later time.

But now, by using Watson's notebooks, old newspaper reports, police files, and other scraps of information which the documents provide, it has been possible to piece together some of Holmes' cases which have never before been published. In each story, actual pages from the notebooks, or other original documents, have been included. They will be found in places where they add some information, provide some illustration, or pick out what may prove to be important clues.

But it is hoped that they also offer something more. By using your imagination, these pages can give **you** the opportunity to relive the challenge, the excitement and, occasionally, the danger which Watson, who tells the stories, must himself have experienced in working with Sherlock Holmes – the man so often described as "the world's greatest detective".

About this Book

Watson met Mary Morstan when he and Holmes first shared the lodgings at Baker Street. Mary had come seeking Holmes' assistance to explain a series of odd events which seemed, in some way, connected with the disappearance of her father, ten years before. So began an investigation which was to uncover a truly tangled web of treachery, murder and mystery. The full account was published under the title, *The Sign of Four*.

It was during that investigation that John Watson and Mary Morstan found themselves to be deeply in love. In 1887 they were married. Watson left Baker Street, purchasing a small practice in the Paddington district. Between his wife and his work, Watson found his life to be blissfully complete and though, usually at Holmes' request, he did assist in a few of his more difficult cases, he was to see less and less of his old friend.

It was only two years after their marriage that Mary contracted tuberculosis, a lingering sickness which at that time would almost certainly prove fatal. Watson could hope only to prolong Mary's life by sending her to spend periods in a sanatorium. It is at such a time that this story begins – for Watson a time of deep sadness. This is, perhaps, the reason why he never formally recorded this case, which is not only generally remarkable, but ended in events as dramatic as any to be found in the annals of Sherlock Holmes.

Chapter One

The Reluctant Client

Though myself a doctor, it was only with the greatest difficulty that I had, at first, been able to accept the idea that Mary, my beloved wife, was a victim of consumption. Now it was beyond any such denial. Her face had assumed that pale transparency of skin which gave her small features an almost elfin quality. Yet I knew it was not the face of immortality, but rather a first pale shadow of death.

That winter, though not so cold as many, had brought with it a rash of London fogs, chilling to the marrow of the bone and yellow with choking, sulphurous fumes, spewed out from London's ever growing forest of smoking chimneys. In January, I had sent Mary to a sanatorium in the mountains of Wales, and though it was now March, I had felt it better that she remain there.

I missed her most desperately whenever she

was gone from me and, on such occasions, sought to escape in my work, my practice having now become of a respectable size. But our periods of separation had never been so long as this. Even my work had ceased to provide any effective distraction and, beginning to fear for my own efficiency as a doctor, I had abandoned the care of my patients to my colleague, Anstruther. It was an act which served only to cast me into a still deeper state of depression and despair.

I had told no-one of Mary's illness, except for my close medical colleagues, though her appearance and her increasing absences from home must by now have cast some doubt upon my explanations that she was staying with friends or relatives. I had told the truth to one other person – Sherlock Holmes.

I was ashamed of the manner in which I'd neglected Holmes since my marriage. Mary had encouraged me to continue my interest in Holmes' work. Anstruther had always been willing to see to the needs of my patients. But I had chosen to live my life with Mary, almost, I felt, to the exclusion of the rest of the world in general, and Holmes in particular.

I set out very early that morning for Baker Street, feeling a desperate need to talk to a friend – and trusting that despite my shameful neglect I did still have one in Sherlock Holmes. The morning, though bright with spring sunshine, was deceptively cold and even the short, brisk walk from

Praed Street to Baker Street, left me wishing that I'd worn an overcoat over my tweed suit. Holmes, who was just finishing breakfast, seemed genuinely delighted to see me. My having refused a stronger remedy against the cold, he insisted upon having Mrs Hudson bring me fresh, hot coffee.

Holmes was standing at the window and, though he was asking me what news I had of Mary, and about the state of my own wellbeing, it was very certain that a part of his attention was concentrated upon something in the street below. Mrs Hudson arrived with the fresh coffee. Holmes left the window to join me at the table.

"I think," he said, refilling his own cup, "that I may have a client. A cab pulled up just below the window at the very moment that Mrs Hudson was letting you into the house. It's still there."

"A man or a woman?" I asked.

"A man, Watson – though all that I've been able to see is his boots, a few inches of trouser leg and a glimpse of one hand as he removed his glove."

"From which," I found myself joking, "you have deduced that the man is six foot two, is on leave from the Indian Army – and has a spaniel called Bob!"

Holmes smiled, broadly.

"I am delighted to hear, Watson, that you have, at least, retained something of your sense of humour. As to my supposed deduction, you may be surprised to know that you are not entirely wrong! The man is short – probably a little over five feet – and therefore too small for the army. He is of comfortable means and in late middle age. He is quick tempered and aggressive in his manner. And since his home is unusually close to the sea, he is obviously a visitor to London."

"You said I was not entirely wrong!"

"You were not, Watson. He *has* a small dog – though I cannot yet be certain of its breed, or its name."

In some nine years of knowing Holmes, I had still not found myself able, unquestioningly, to accept his seemingly more extravagant deductions. This certainly sounded to be one of them.

"You look disbelieving, Watson. It is a matter easily proved. As you can hear, we already have an impatient knocking on the front door. While I change from my dressing gown, be a good fellow and answer it – before Mrs Hudson has the opportunity to send our visitor away."

Holmes claimed never to be at his best in the early morning and did have a rule, occasionally broken, to see no-one before eleven without an appointment. I had come to Baker Street early, wishing only for a quiet talk with Holmes and thinking it a time when we were least likely to be disturbed by the arrival of a client. But my curiosity had been unexpectedly aroused. Nor could I now deny an ungenerous hope – that Holmes might, for once, be proved wrong!

....

Nathan Pierce stood no more than five foot two. That included whatever extra height was provided by boots which were skilfully, but still visibly, built up at the heels. He was well dressed, looked to be in his early fifties and, while not actually impolite, had a brusqueness of manner which conveyed that impression. It had required Holmes' insistence to persuade him to hand his hat, his gloves and his stick to me, and seat himself in a chair. His stated preference had been to remain standing.

He removed a gold watch from his waistcoat pocket, flicked open its cover, snapped it shut with a loud click, and returned it to the pocket, in a series of quick, almost flamboyant gestures which suggested that time was a matter of some importance to him. It was the second time he had done it since entering the room.

"The matter which brings me here, Mr Holmes, is really quite trifling. For that, I apologise. Had there been any way of dealing with it, other than by calling upon you without appointment, and at this early hour of the morning, be assured that I would have used it. I can, at least, promise you that I shall be brief."

That, Holmes told him, would be appreciated.

"Very well," Pierce continued. "At some time between now –" He consulted his watch for a third time. "– and eleven this morning, you may be visited by a young woman. She may *not* give her real name. But it is Emily Pierce. The girl is my ward. You will, however, have no difficulty in recognising her. She is quite small, has blonde hair and blue eyes. She will be wearing a dress of a quite striking blue colour, and a matching hat with white ostrich feathers on it."

He paused.

"Your description would seem more than adequate," Holmes assured him. "Please continue."

"If I appeared to hesitate, Mr Holmes, it was only because I am unable, with any certainty, to predict the girl's manner. It may appear calm. Equally, she may appear to be deeply distressed. Whichever it is, the reason she will give for wishing to see you, will be one which you would find to be most persuasive."

"Am I to know this reason?"

"In as many words, Mr Holmes, my ward will tell you that she comes to you for help, because she is in fear for her life. That much I tell you, since you may hear it from the girl herself. But you will see that there is no necessity for you to know more, when I tell you that the girl's fear exists only in her imagination. It is a matter which does not require your professional assistance, and could not possibly benefit from it."

"And the purpose of your visit, this morning, was to tell me that?"

"That, Mr Holmes – and to make a request. I assume, in view of what I've told you, that you wouldn't, in any case, wish to see my ward. It would, however, be of assistance to me if the reason she were given for your not seeing her, was that you are not at home, and will not be returning to London for several days."

Holmes didn't reply. He was leaning back in his chair, with his eyes closed, elbows resting on the arms of the chair and his hands touching lightly at the fingertips. It was an attitude he frequently adopted when deep in thought, but one which appeared to be causing Pierce some irritation. He consulted his watch yet again, before finally voicing his impatience.

"It was a simple request, Mr Holmes. As the girl's guardian, I have the right to decide what she may or may not do – and I do not wish you to see her. Give *her* whatever reason you like. Just give *me* the assurance that you will not see her, and I can leave you."

Holmes opened his eyes and stared hard at his fingertips.

"You misinterpret my hesitation, Mr Pierce. It is not a matter of reasons, rather one of whether I am prepared to give you any kind of assurance whatsoever."

Pierce's face had visibly coloured up, but Holmes forestalled anything he might have been about to say. "I've heard you out, Mr Pierce . Now do me that same courtesy.

"You come here without appointment. You tell me that a young woman may call upon me, asking for my help, because she is in fear for her life. You are not certain what name she will give, but you tell me that her real name is Emily Pierce, and that she is your ward. You tell me also that the girl's fears are imaginary, and that I am to send her away – unheard. Am I accurate in my summary?"

"You are, and I still do not see any reason for your hesitation in giving me an assurance to which I am fully entitled under the law of this land."

"To which you are surely entitled," Holmes replied, "if you are Nathan Pierce, if the girl is your ward, if her fears are, as you say, only imaginary – and if what you ask is not, in truth, intended to further some crime. Let us say, the death of a young woman who is desperately seeking my help."

Pierce opened and closed his mouth several times, but no words came out.

"I'm sorry if I shock you, but it was necessary to make my point. What I suggest may be unlikely, but not impossible. Your own account, Mr Pierce, is itself unusual – though one which I might have accepted but for two inconsistencies which I find curious."

"And those are?" The words were abrupt.

"You said that you would not have come here if you could have dealt with the matter in some other way. If you knew that your ward might come here, but no later than eleven o'clock, then you could have waited in the street and waylaid her."

"And the other?"

"You describe a young woman who, for what-ever reason, is in a highly disturbed state of mind, who should not, I would have thought, be wandering alone on the streets of London. Yet your only concern, if she comes here, is that I should send her away!"

Pierce moved his hand towards his waistcoat pocket, as if once more to remove his watch, but the hand never reached the pocket. He placed it, instead, across his eyes, at the same time, bowing his head in what could equally have been an attitude either of defeat, or of despair. When he did, at last, remove his hand and lift his head, it was almost as though a mask had dropped from the face. The look of confidence was gone. Even the voice had changed, sounding almost pleading as he said, "I need your help, Mr Holmes. I could explain – but there is no time! If Emily finds me here, it will defeat the very purpose for which I came."

Holmes answered in a tone which might have conveyed some feeling of sympathy, but in words which could leave Pierce in no doubt of his un-changed resolve to be satisfied of the reasonable-ness of what had been asked of him. "Your choice is simple, Mr Pierce. You leave now, without your assurance, or you remain for long enough to tell the whole story. As to the arrival of your ward, there is a room next to this which will, if need be, afford you concealment."

It was obvious that Pierce now felt himself to have no choice. He began once more, this time in a subdued and quite hesitant fashion, in striking contrast to his manner upon his first arrival.

Nathan Pierce was the older of two brothers. He described himself as a confirmed bachelor and one who preferred his own company. Being of independent means, he had chosen to live in a place which gave him a secluded life. He had purchased a house on the Cornish coast, quite near to a busy fishing port, but built out on a peninsular in a manner which provided complete privacy. His brother, Joseph, had married, and had a child, Emily. Three years ago, both Joseph and his wife had been lost at sea when the ship the SS *China Star* had sunk with all hands, in a storm off the Cape of Good Hope. I well remembered the tragedy being widely reported in the newspapers of the time.

Under the terms of Joseph's will, Nathan had become Emily's guardian, and trustee of a not inconsiderable fortune – which the girl would inherit upon reaching the age of twenty-one. The guardianship had not, at first, presented Nathan Pierce with any problems. At the time of her parents' deaths, Emily had been at finishing school in Switzerland, and had expressed a preference to remain there.

"Of course, Mr Holmes, that could not be for ever. Emily visited me for the occasion of her twentieth birthday, and decided to remain. I do not consider my home a very suitable place for a young woman. It is, as I've said, isolated. Some would call it gloomy, even frightening. But that was Emily's wish, and in a year, having gained her inheritance, she would become totally independent, and would be free to choose to live wherever she pleased.

"I did my best, Mr Holmes. I had no experience of the needs of a young woman, but I anticipated that the greatest problem might be boredom. I took her on· quite frequent visits to Penzance, Plymouth and Exeter, and she often accompanied me on my trips to London, which I visit perhaps once a month. I even bought her a small dog. It's very attached to her, though not she to it. I think that I've become rather more attached to the animal myself. But, in short, Mr Holmes, I failed."

Within three months of her arrival, Emily had changed – in no dramatic way, but enough for Pierce to sense that something was troubling her. After much persuasion, she had confessed to having a strange and frightening, recurrent dream. In the dream, it was the day of her twenty-first birthday – and there was a party. Her mother and father were there, her uncle Nathan, and several of her friends from her school in Switzerland. But it was not like any ordinary party. Everyone was dressed in black. Her mother, and some of her school friends, looked as if they had been crying. No-one spoke to Emily, and when she tried to speak to them, they completely ignored her, just as though she wasn't there. Then, still in her dream, she shouted at them, "Why won't you speak to me! It's my birthday. You look as if you were at a funeral!" At that, all the guests turned to face her – and her father said, "It *is* a funeral Emily. It's yours." Always, at that point, she woke – naturally very frightened.

"I didn't take her dream too seriously, Mr Holmes, thinking it might be delayed shock at her parents' deaths, and living in a place which could well give rise to morbid fancies in a young woman. But the fancies moved out of the dreams into Emily's waking world. She began to see and hear things which had no real existence. Ridiculous as it may sound, she became convinced that she was going to die on her twenty-first birthday. And you must also understand my increasing difficulty in keeping all this from the servants!"

"But it must have occurred to you to seek medical help," I suggested.

"It did, Doctor Watson. On the advice of a friend, I brought Emily to London, and without giving her any forewarning, took her to see some man called Forbes."

"Dr Steven Forbes of Harley Street?"

"The same."

"A good man," I said, "the best in his field."

"I didn't find him so, Doctor. He talked at great length about what he called 'female hysterias'. But his only practical suggestion was to commit

Emily to a private institution for treatment – a
madhouse, Doctor Watson! The Pierces are an old
and respectable family. Their past has not been
entirely without some breath of scandal, but
never the disgrace of insanity! You must see I
could do nothing but take Emily home again."

Holmes was looking slightly bemused, perhaps
because Pierce did sound to have been more concerned about the servants and the family name,
than he was about his ward's condition. It was no
surprise to me. The idea that disorders of the
mind were, at best, not respectable, at worst,
some visitation of the Devil, may seem quite
medieval, but was one I'd encountered several
times, even in my own practice. I was none the
less curious to know what Pierce had done next.

"Nothing, Doctor Watson, and you may find
this no less extraordinary than I did myself –
indeed it took me some days to realise, and longer
to believe it. From the moment of leaving Harley
Street, Emily's behaviour had become, in every
way, normal! No more imaginings – not even, she
assured me, bad dreams. And so it has continued,
Mr Holmes. I can only guess a reason – perhaps
she realised that the man I'd taken her to see was
no ordinary physician, or she may even have
overheard his advice that I have her committed to
an institution. The reason seemed unimportant. I
have spent three normal, I might even say
'happy', months with my ward. It was, therefore,
no surprise to me when, the day before yesterday,

she asked if she might come with me on my trip to London – to do some shopping, she said. I agreed, most readily."

"But, clearly, something unexpected has happened."

"This morning, Mr Holmes, as we left the Great Western Hotel, Emily was speaking to a cab driver. I caught just two words – 'Sherlock Holmes'. To my knowledge, Mr Holmes, your name has been mentioned only once before – by me. It was just before our visit to Forbes. Emily had been insisting, again, that she had seen intruders in the house. I fear I lost my patience. I asked her what she wished me to do. The police would certainly laugh at me. Should I, perhaps, call in Sherlock Holmes, the famous London detective?

"You can imagine my thoughts, Mr Holmes! Was Emily *not* cured? Had she merely been deceiving me? And what was I to do? If I was wrong, then might I, unwittingly, do or say something to revive those fears which I so dearly hoped had gone? If I was right, and I were suddenly to forbid her to do her shopping alone, or as you suggested waylay her in Baker Street, might it serve only to confirm her fears?"

"As might I," Holmes added, "if I were to hear and believe her story. I have only two more questions. Why will your ward not come after eleven o'clock?"

"Because, at around midday, we should be on

the train returning to Cornwall. I am only praying that Emily will be on it!"

"And why do you wish her to be told that I am not at home and will not be returning for several days?"

"It was not important. I thought it might prevent her returning here today – or even attempting to return to London alone. You see, Mr Holmes, I still cling to one last hope. Emily's twenty-first birthday is in four days' time. If that time passes, and she finds herself still alive, then that must surely put an end to any ridiculous imaginings. What else can I tell you?"

"Nothing," was Holmes' answer. "I do appreciate that my insistence upon hearing your full story must have caused you some pain and embarrassment. I trust that you appreciate my reasons for that insistence. You have my assurance, Mr Pierce – and I will delay you no longer. I'm sure that Dr Watson will accompany you to the street and ensure that you are not seen by your ward, should she indeed have decided to come here."

I took Pierce to the street door, advising him to stay within the doorway until I had hailed a cab. With no-one in sight who resembled Pierce's description of his ward, I hurried him into the cab and saw it drive off before returning upstairs. Holmes was standing by the chair where Pierce had sat – holding in his hand, a gold pocket watch.

"I found it in the chair, Watson."

It had to be Pierce's watch. The number of times he'd had it in and out of his pocket, it was little wonder that it had come loose from its chain. Holmes was holding the watch out towards me. "Tell me what you see, Watson."

"A watch – obviously! It's gold – a half hunter – looks expensive. What else should I see?"

"Principally, Watson, that Mr Pierce was carrying two watches. And I find myself asking, 'Why?'."

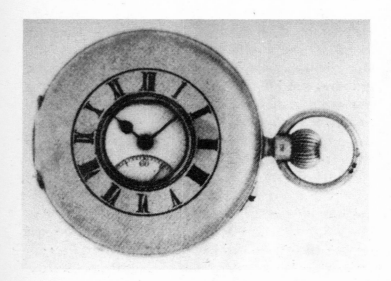

Author's Addition – A "half hunter" gold watch similar to that found by Holmes, and described later in more detail.

Chapter Two

The Girl in the Blue Dress

Holmes had moved into the better light afforded by the window and, with the aid of his magnifying glass, was examining Pierce's watch – for what reason I didn't know. But, since it appeared that every part of both its case and its mechanism was about to be the subject of careful scrutiny, I supposed that it might take him some time. I crossed the room to the bookshelves.

"Still in its usual place, Watson – bottom shelf, five from the right."

Holmes' eyes were still fixed on the glass, his attitude one of intense concentration. Yet he had neither failed to notice my movement nor, it seemed, deduce my purpose. The fifth book from the right on the bottom shelf was Bradshaw's *Railway Timetable* – the very thing I had intended to find! Two minutes later, Holmes had put down his glass and pocketed the watch.

"Tell me then," he said, "what time is the train from Paddington to Penzance?"

I told him, 11.46. "I'm sorry," I added. "I thought that you'd become so engrossed in that watch that you'd forgotten the more pressing matter of how we might seek to return it before our visitor leaves London –"

"– since he's left us with no address. No, Watson, I had not forgotten. Indeed my haste to carry out the examination was for the very reason that if I am wrong, I might not have the opportunity to do so again."

I would have asked, "Wrong about what?", had he not immediately removed Pierce's watch from his pocket and said, "This one gives the time as seventeen minutes past ten."

I looked at my watch and agreed that that was the time – though I did wonder why Holmes had not consulted his own watch.

"Then tell me, Watson. You have clearly been giving consideration to the matter. What is our best course of action? We have six alternatives."

I told him that it had crossed my mind to wait until eleven. If Emily Pierce did call, then the watch could be returned to her – but that would not be possible without giving away the fact that we had already been visited by her guardian. I had then thought that the most certain way was to go to Paddington Station, perhaps a half hour before the train was due to leave. That way, we would be certain to see Pierce before he boarded the train – but we could be faced with much the same problem as arose with the first solution. Emily would be with him. It would be easy to invent some story about finding the watch, but both our faces had appeared so often in the pages of the *Strand Magazine*, it was not impossible that the girl might recognise one or both of us.

I took Holmes' silence to mean that he agreed with all I had said so far, and felt confident to continue.

"Pierce said that they were staying at the Great Western Hotel. Since it is next to Paddington Station, I imagine that neither they nor their luggage will leave the hotel until shortly before the train leaves. If, therefore, we were to give the watch to one of the hotel staff, then they could return it, saying simply that it had been dropped in the hotel. But *you* said 'six' alternatives, Holmes. I'm afraid that's only three."

"No matter, Watson. Your reasoning is quite excellent, and your last suggestion is precisely the one which I wanted to hear. Let us waste no time in carrying it out!"

I had wanted to hear the other three alternatives – and to tell Holmes that, since it was now only ten thirty, I saw no need for unreasonable haste. But Holmes was already making for the door.

"I must instruct Mrs Hudson upon what she must say if Emily Pierce does arrive in our absence. Meanwhile, Watson, if you look in my bedroom, I think that you will find several rugs. Since you were complaining of the cold when you arrived, take one to place over your legs in the cab."

Having hailed a cab, I boarded it first, expecting Holmes to follow me. He did not. For some reason, he had chosen to remain on the pavement until he had given his instructions to the driver – which did seem to be a little unnecessary when he had only to tell him that we were going to the Great Western Hotel. It was not something to which I had given a second thought until, having turned into Crawford Street, we turned almost immediately left again at Gloucester Place – no longer travelling in the direction of Paddington, but back in the direction from which we'd come!

"Nothing is wrong, Watson. The driver is doing no more than carry out the instructions which I gave him. We *are* going to Paddington – but not until I have satisfied what you may call my curiosity. That is why I rushed you out of the house with what you may have thought unnecessary haste."

We left Gloucester Place at George Street, and were back in Baker Street itself. I had thought that we must be returning to 221B but, just before we had reached the Union Assurance Offices on the corner of King Street, we stopped – less than a hundred yards short of it.

I was not at all certain why it had been necessary to circle three streets merely to come back to the spot where we were. If, as I assumed, Holmes' purpose was to observe the arrival of Emily

Pierce, and from a position where we were unlikely to be seen, it would have been much easier to have gone up Baker Street, turned about in the road, and waited, perhaps opposite to the Baker Street Bazaar. We would have had a better view of 221B. As it was, that view was frequently blocked by traffic in and out of King Street. I had thought to say something about it, but decided I would

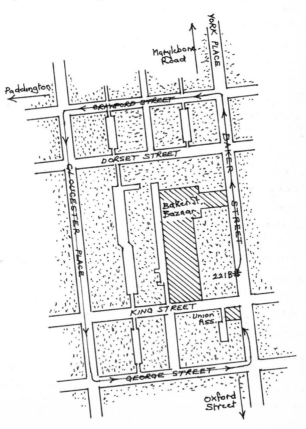

not. Even with Holmes' rug about my legs, I was already feeling cold – and I had started to wonder what I was doing there at all! I'd come to Baker Street that morning, wanting only to talk to Holmes about my own problems. Suddenly, it was as if I was back again, working with Holmes on a case – except that there was no case! He had just admitted that he was merely satisfying his curiosity. Perhaps, having returned the watch, that would be an end of it – and I might still succeed in having that talk between old friends – which was all that I wanted!

"You seem remarkably silent, Watson!"

I said that I was cold.

"I'm sorry. I confess that I am not too warm my-self – though we should not have long to wait. But talking will take your mind off it. Tell me how I knew as much about Pierce before he had entered the room."

I'd forgotten how much Holmes' ego thrived upon an appreciative and suitably astonished audience. My hands and feet were becoming quite numb and, at that precise moment, I felt that I owed Holmes nothing – except, possibly, the responsibility for an outbreak of painful chil-blains!

"I thought it a little obvious," I said. "The size of the man's feet and hand, and the built-up heels of the boots, told you about his height. The built-up boots also told you that he was self conscious about his height. People with such feelings of inferiority frequently overcompensate by adopting an aggressive attitude. The quality of the boots and the material of the trousers suggested that he was comfortably off. The style of the boots, the choice of material, and possibly the hand, gave some indication of his age.

"As to his living close to the sea, the boots had some white marks around the edge of the uppers – though they had clearly been recently blackened and polished, probably overnight in the hotel. It rained through the night. There were still pools of water about when I left home. The white marks were salt. Once salt has impregnated the leather, and no matter how often boots are cleaned, they have only to get wet for the salt once more to come to the surface."

I knew that Holmes had probably made those same deductions in seconds. It had taken me many minutes and I should have felt a little mean in describing them as "obvious". What I did feel, was rather proud of myself – particularly for the bit about the salt! Holmes' gaze had been fixed in the direction of 221B. He did not shift it when he said, "And what about the small dog?"

I had forgotten about the dog! I suddenly felt cheated. I had looked for hairs on Pierce's trousers. I had looked for marks on his boots where a dog might have scuffed the leather with its claws. I had looked for scars of scratches or bites on his hands. I had even looked for the white traces which a dog's saliva can leave on dark cloth.

There were none. But I was saved from having to admit my defeat!

"Look, Watson. Our second visitor has arrived!"

A young woman was stepping down from a cab, immediately in front of 221B. Though my view was interrupted by both the King Street traffic and by pedestrians on the pavement, there was no mistaking that flash of quite brilliant blue. She crossed to the door of 221B and knocked on it. I noticed that the cab remained. I could tell by her attitude that the door had been opened and that she was in conversation with Mrs Hudson. Holmes raised the stick he was carrying and did no more with it than raise the trap above our heads and let it drop. It was clearly some pre-arranged signal – since we had now begun to move forward again – though quite slowly.

As we reached the opposite corner of King Street, I could see the girl's blonde hair and the white ostrich feathers in the hat. I was wishing that she would move her head so that I might see her face when, quite suddenly, she did turn completely about – looking, it seemed, towards the driver of the cab which had brought her. It was done with a quickness of movement which suggested that something had startled her. As if to confirm that impression, she gave only one brief glance back towards 221B before swiftly remounting the cab, and was instantly driven off with surprising speed.

Holmes had again lifted the trap above us. "You know what to do," he shouted, "but remember, driver, that it is not our purpose to catch him – only to make him believe that we are trying!"

It was not a time to be asking questions! Having been thrown hard back in my seat, my full attention was concentrated upon remaining in it as our cab swayed wildly from side to side as we weaved in and out of other vehicles at what I felt to be a quite reckless pace!

I was conscious of our having passed from Baker Street into York Place and was thinking that we would have to stop before we reached the busy Marylebone Road – when we did! I had a brief vision of our horse, rearing at the suddenness with which it had been brought to a halt. My hat was immediately tipped over my eyes, and I would most certainly have slid to the floor but for Holmes' swiftness in grasping the back of my jacket. I was about to suggest that our driver was a madman, but one glance at Holmes' face told me that any protest on my part would merely be words wasted. I had recognised the look – something between elation and triumph – where Holmes' mind was closed to anything other than the excitement of the moment and the satisfaction of having just proved himself right! "Look, Watson! Look!" was all he said to me.

There were two lines of cabs in front of us, the one carrying the girl at the front of the line nearer to the centre of the road. Several cabs had just passed on our side of the Marleybone Road, with a small gap between them and a horse-drawn omnibus which followed them. The front cab in the line nearer to the pavement, was moving to slip into the gap, but so was the cab alongside it – the one carrying the girl. It looked impossible for both cabs to slip into the small gap! The drivers of the omnibus and of the cab nearer the pavement clearly thought the same. Both took avoiding action – the cab mounting the pavement, while the driver of the omnibus swung his horses towards the centre of the road. The result of the latter was that several of the omnibus passengers on the open upper deck suddenly vanished, while those still able rose to their feet with their fists shaking! Everything on the busy crossing was brought to a temporary halt – except the cab carrying the girl, which had passed completely from sight. Holmes started to laugh! Still laughing, he again raised the trap above us. "Well done, driver! Now take us to the Great Western Hotel."

The rest of the short journey was quiet, but what I had already experienced convinced me that there might be a better place and time to discover its purpose!

At the reception desk of the Great Western, a young man of a smart and cheerful appearance instantly confirmed that a Mr Pierce and his ward were staying at the hotel – both, he added, and Mr Nathan Pierce in particular, being among their regular patrons. He remembered seeing them earlier that morning, but not since. If we would care to seat ourselves in the reception hall, and to wait, he would discover whether their luggage was still in their rooms.

We had waited for some time before he beckoned us back to the desk. Apologising for the delay, he explained that their luggage was not in their rooms, and that he had had the public rooms paged for them – without success. But, he explained, that did not mean that they would not be returning to the hotel. Many guests had their luggage transferred to the hotel's luggage room, early on the morning of their departure. They merely had it picked up from there by a porter, at whatever time was convenient for it to be taken to their train. But, without knowing the numbers which had been placed on the luggage, there was no simple means of knowing whether it was there. "You must appreciate, gentlemen, that we have one hundred and three bedrooms, all of which are usually occupied."

It was now 11.15. It might be that our only chance of finding Pierce was to wait for him on the station platform, but there remained the problem of Emily being with him. I explained to the young man at reception that our purpose was merely to return a watch which Mr Pierce had dropped from his pocket. If we could be given his address, that might be the simplest means of returning it. I should have known the answer. It was not the policy of the hotel to give the address of any of its clients. But they would undertake to post the watch for us or, if we were to leave our address, they would write to Mr Pierce, so that he might make his own arrangements. While I thought that either of those alternatives sounded satisfactory, Holmes clearly did not. He said that we might take advantage of the kind offer, but only if we failed to find Mr Pierce before the train left – and with that, almost bundled me out of the hotel.

I had had enough of Holmes' unpredictable behaviour for one morning and wasn't going to give him the satisfaction of entering into some kind of argument. The result of that, was that we spent a cold half hour on a draughty platform of Paddington Station, with little exchange of conversation between us.

The 11.46 left on time. Pierce and his ward were not on it. If I thought I could read anything from the expression on Holmes' face, it was that he was pleased! *I* would now have returned to the hotel but since it was clearly one of those times where Holmes was enjoying being both perverse and mysterious, it did not surprise me when he announced that we were returning to Baker Street.

I had almost forgotten that we had yet to hear what had passed between Emily Pierce and Mrs Hudson during the girl's brief visit to 221B. It proved to be little more than we either knew, or might have expected. She had introduced herself as Emily Pierce and asked to see Holmes, "upon a matter of great urgency". She had been told, as instructed, that Mr Holmes was away from home and would not be returning for several days. Mrs Hudson had then asked her if she wished to leave some message, or an address where Mr Holmes might contact her. She had answered that she feared it would be "too late". "I think she might have said more, excepting that just then, something seemed to startle her. It might have been a shout, but I 'd not be sure of that, Mr Holmes, not with all the noise the traffic was making. All I can say for sure is that all of a sudden she turns herself right about – as if she was looking for somebody. At any event, Mr Holmes, she didn't do no more after that than give a quick look back, before she's into the cab she's come in – and she's off."

Holmes asked if Mrs Hudson had noticed anything unusual about the girl's appearance or manner. Did she appear nervous? "I couldn't be saying she wasn't. White she was, and you might say trembling – though I'd say it was more like shaking with the cold. A very pretty dress she had on – and I'd think wanting everybody to see it. But you can tell the girl's got no mother!"

What might have seemed a surprising deduction on the part of Mrs Hudson was not. Holmes had told her as much. And it's purpose was merely to introduce a piece of Mrs Hudson's homespun philosophy on the virtues of sensible clothing, and how those young women foolish enough to ignore them, were doing no more than "store up trouble for themselves in later life".

As a doctor, I agreed, but was quite glad when Mrs Hudson did, at last, leave us. Holmes seated himself in his chair, and I hoped that we might now have some conversation, but he began, once more, to contemplate Pierce's watch – which, notably, we had failed to return. I was, therefore, half surprised when he did decide to address me.

"You are wondering, Watson, why I have been behaving as if I were investigating some mystery when I sense that you are by no means convinced that there is any mystery to investigate."

He had expressed my thoughts exactly.

"It is because of several things," he continued. "Why Pierce should wait so long in the cab before he came into the house, the girl's dress, the timing of her arrival, her behaviour, and that of her cab driver, the absence of both Pierce and the girl from the hotel and their failure to be on the train, and," he added, pausing in a manner which suggested that he considered it to be of some special significance, "this watch."

"You say, Holmes, that the watch is not the one Pierce had in his pocket. You obviously saw the one in his pocket. I didn't. It was always covered by his hand."

"Not 'saw', Watson – 'heard'. You remember his frequent and extravagant gestures in consulting it – as if we might be meant to notice something, like the loud click as he closed the case before returning it to his pocket. The watch I am holding is a half hunter, the purpose of the small glass being –"

I finished the sentence for him, "that it makes it unnecessary to open the case to read the time! So the man *was* carrying two watches. But I see no mystery in that. He had just collected it from the repairers."

"No, Watson. There are traces of fluff caught in the hinges and a hair twisted around the stem of the winder. And this watch has never been re-paired. Nowhere are there any marks of a watch-maker's tools, and a watchmaker always scratches a small mark on the inside of the case to show when and where it was repaired. This case is unmarked."

"Then he was taking it to be repaired."

"Then why, Watson, is it near fully wound and, as you confirmed, showing the correct time?"

I had no more suggestions. I told Holmes that he must explain the mystery.

"I can't, Watson – not with certainty. I am cer-tain that none of this affair is what it appears but, as yet, I cannot make the pieces fit together.

"But let us speak no more of Nathan Pierce for today. Already, I have sadly neglected my duties as a friend. You came this morning to talk to me, Watson – and all I have done is to try your patience. Do me the kindness of remaining for lunch and I will promise you my full attention."

Pages from Watson's notebooks

Pierce had waited because he saw Holmes had a visitor. I didn't understand what he meant about "the time of her arrival" — but as to her behaviour, that appeared to me quite normal — for a young woman in the kind of mental state which her guardian had described. Holmes probably found parts of Pierce's story to be very strange but, as a doctor who has taken some interest in mental afflictions, I could see that he was merely describing the symptoms of a recognised form of mental disorder.

The ways in which Pierce had reacted to these symptoms may not have appeared very wise — though I would say they were not unusual for any ordinary person suddenly faced with strange, and sometimes, quite frightening behaviour.

I think that the girl did no more than suddenly take fright in

Baker Street — and in her state of mind, could well have felt quite terrified when she realised that she was being followed. It was most probably that which stopped her from returning to the hotel. I've no doubt that Pierce didn't catch the 11.46 because he'd had to go looking for her!

I'm sure that Holmes is wrong about the watch. There must be a dozen perfectly good reasons why a man is carrying two watches.

Must ask Holmes how he knew about Pierce's dog!

Chapter Three

The Last Alternative

It was early evening before I left Baker Street. I could not say that I was happy. But I did feel that I had lost something of the sense of utter wretchedness with which I had set out that morning.

Holmes was not a man to whom I would have gone had my purpose been to seek sympathy. There was a gentler side to his character – and I was perhaps among the few people ever to have seen it. I did not expect to see it on this occasion – nor did I. An eavesdropper upon our conversation that afternoon might have described some of the things which he said to me as almost "brutal". But in that, they would have been wrong. Holmes did only what I had been unable to do for myself – made me face up to the stark realities of the situation in which I had found myself. It was what I expected, and the very reason that I had sought his counsel.

Much of what he had said to me, I had said to myself a hundred times – with little effect. Hearing those same things said by another person – especially a person whom one respects as much as I did Holmes, can be very different. I knew that it was of no help either to myself, or to my wife, Mary, that I should wallow in self pity, while she fought so bravely. I had now determined to pick up the pieces of my life, beginning perhaps with a return to my practice and to the care of my patients. There had been a time when my involvement with Holmes and his investigations totally outweighed my every other interest, even medicine. But that was before my marriage, and memories of those days were nowhere in my mind as I returned that evening to Praed Street. It seemed, therefore, as unaccountable as it was surprising, that I found myself, late that night, getting out my notebook and setting down my thoughts on the morning's events just as I might have done in the six years when I had lodged at 221B Baker Street!

....

It was my intention the next morning to see Anstruther and to tell him that I was no longer in need of his generous services. I was, in fact, leaving the house upon that errand and had opened the street door – only to find Holmes on my doorstep! I was sufficiently glad to see him, not to make any immediate enquiry as to the purpose of his visit. I took the opportunity to express my gratitude for the good which had come of our conversation on the previous day and – though mainly in jest, but to prove the extent of my near return to normality – showed him the notes I had made. He insisted upon reading them.

"Remarkable!" was his first comment. "This serves to confirm my own thinking exactly. It seems as if every part of Pierce's story which it has been so far possible to check, serves either to confirm that story, or leaves us with a question. And always there are two possible answers to the question. You, Watson, have written down one possible set of answers. Take them together and they lead to only one conclusion. Pierce was telling the truth and your instincts, Watson, were right. There is no mystery."

The implication of what Holmes had said was clear. He had found a quite different set of answers to those questions – but why did he seem so unsure of himself? That was not like Holmes!

"Because, my friend, they lead to no conclusion of which I can make any sense. I am therefore wrong, or there is a piece of the puzzle which is still missing – which is why I am here this morning."

I had no idea what Holmes had in mind, but said that if there was any way I could help –

"I think you can, Watson. When we were considering how the watch might be returned, I spoke of six alternatives. One was merely to wait for Pierce to contact me. I have reason to believe that he would – but it would be too late for my purposes. We failed yesterday to obtain his address from the Great Western Hotel. But there remains another source – Forbes."

I knew of Steven Forbes by reputation. I had met him once, briefly, after a lecture which he gave at University College upon Professor Freud's theories on neurotic affections. So I hardly knew the man and, as I told Holmes, it would, in any case, be unethical for him to give me the address of one of his patients.

"You make my point, Watson. In your present circumstances, I would not have bothered you with a matter which did not demand a considerable degree of ingenuity – and which I could not possibly accomplish myself. I do need your help, old friend."

I did not fail to recognise Holmes at his most persuasive, nor did I suppose I would be able to refuse! I asked how urgent it was. With Holmes, I should have known that the answer would be "today"!

....

I abandoned my plan to see Anstruther and went straightway to Harley Street. Forbes had already begun on his appointments for the day. It was not like a general practice. Forbes' appointments were at hourly intervals and many patients would be there for the whole of that time. It was possible that he might find a few minutes, between patients, to see me, but preferred that I return at four in the afternoon, when he would certainly be free.

It was very much against my principles, deliberately to deceive a medical colleague into breaking the code of professional ethics, and I could only do so by means of a lie – that Pierce had come to me, seeking my assistance as a doctor. In such an event, it would be ethical for me to consult with Forbes as someone from whom Pierce had already sought advice.

It was not, at the time, something of which I could feel proud, but I have to say that it was a deception which worked well. I arrived at Harley Street, for my four o'clock appointment, still uncertain upon what pretext I was going to ask for the address of someone who I claimed to be my own patient! The problem was solved by Forbes giving me sight of his file – and because he was genuinely concerned about Emily Pierce, he also gave me a good deal of information of a kind which I had not expected. My mission had, undoubtedly, been highly successful but, as I arrived at Baker Street at a little before five, it was with the feeling that the news I carried would prove to be a considerable disappointment to Holmes.

....

"It certainly leaves me in no doubt as to the truth of Pierce's story," I told him. "Forbes was convinced of the seriousness of the girl's mental condition. He'd done more than 'suggest' that Pierce should have Emily committed to an institution. He'd pleaded with him to do so, in the interests of the girl's own safety."

"Tell me, Watson. Did he say who had done most of the talking – Pierce, or his ward?"

"In fact, he did. The girl said very little – but she denied nothing of what her guardian had said to Forbes in her presence.

"I know what's in your mind, Holmes. You suggested to Pierce that he might be asking you to become party to the girl's death. I assume that if the girl were to die, then Pierce would inherit her fortune. I thought your suggestion to be unlikely then. Since my visit to Forbes, I'm now certain that if Pierce *were* seeking to have the girl's inheritance, he must have known that he had no *need* to kill her. He need only have had her committed to an institution as a person of unsound mind. In those circumstances, the law would have given him control of the girl's inheritance. But we know that Pierce did not choose to take advantage of it!"

Holmes was energetically poking at the fire, though it seemed to be burning perfectly well.

"You said, Watson, that Forbes had pleaded with Pierce to have the girl committed, and the words you used were, 'in the interests of the girl's own safety'. Exactly what did you understand him to mean?"

I admitted that I hadn't needed to understand. Forbes had been quite specific. It was not unknown in such cases for the victim to attempt suicide, and he said that he'd made that very plain to Pierce.

Holmes put the poker back in its place. "I'm greatly obliged to you, Watson. Then it is, as I suspected, the last alternative." I watched as he removed Pierce's watch from his pocket. "You see, Watson, it is just as well that we kept the invitation. How long will it take you to pack?"

I'd heard that last question but chose to ignore it, at least until I had understood something more of what Holmes was talking about. I had supposed that my visiting Forbes *was* the sixth and "last alternative". And what was "the invitation"?

"I had not meant to confuse you, Watson. *You* suggested three ways of returning the watch. *My* fourth was to do nothing but wait for Pierce to contact me. My fifth was to use the post, having obtained the address from whatever source. My sixth, and last, was to return the watch in person. I described the watch as an 'invitation', because that is what I believe it is – and why it was deliberately left behind. If we go –" He paused to look at the paper on which I had written Pierce's address. "to Morwella Cove, then the watch is meant to provide us with a convenient means of making our presence there known to Mr Nathan Pierce.

"I know that you still doubt me, Watson – but I will give you three good reasons why you should agree to come with me. Despite your doubts, the affair has already roused your curiosity. Why else did you sit down last night and make your notes?

Why else, but a moment ago, did you not instantly react to my question? You knew very well what I was suggesting.

"I told you yesterday that your greatest problem was self pity. I told you that if you did not find other things to occupy your mind, you would destroy yourself. Give me just three days of your time and I might well provide your mind with a distraction it could never find in a thousand of your patients!"

"You said 'three' good reasons."

"Ah! Watson. The best is always kept till last. In all the years that we have known each other, can you tell me that you have never wished that perhaps, just one time, that it was John H. Watson who proved to be right – and not Sherlock Holmes? If you have any faith in your own judgement, Watson, then believe me when I say that this might be that 'one time'!"

. . . .

In general, I found railway journeys to be both pleasant and relaxing, but not when they lasted for almost ten hours, and took place through the night in freezing temperatures. The newly installed gas lighting in the compartments certainly was less smelly than the old rape-oil lamps, but whistled and plopped in a quite disconcerting manner, even when turned down. It might be said that it did not prevent sleep. That was already made impossible by the cold! We were supplied with freshly filled tin bottles of hot water at each stop, so that we might tuck them beneath our rugs. But with most stops at intervals of some two hours what small comfort they did afford, was short lived.

We had left Paddington at eight the night before with little time to prepare for the journey. Since we were travelling on the mail train, which did not stop at Gallowhill Junction, we had to alight at St Austell. There we waited for a connection to Gallowhill before we could finally board the train for Morwella Halt. After a cold, sleepless night and having watched the breaking of a grey dawn from two unheated station waiting rooms, I felt that things could get no worse. I could not have foreseen that the train to Morwella Halt would smell so strongly of less than fresh herring!

I have but small recollection of our arrival at Morwella Cove, other than that we found rooms at a modest inn, The Fisherman's Rest. Holmes suggested that I might feel better for a good breakfast. I was not only tired but, thanks to the herring, I felt slightly sick. I informed Holmes that doctors required rest as much as fishermen and that I intended to stay in my room and attempt to have some sleep!

I think, to my surprise, I did sleep – quite soundly until almost eleven that morning. Though still feeling less than fully recovered, my conscience prompted me to go downstairs and discover what had become of Holmes. As I'd expected, he was out, but had left a message that I would most likely find him by St Mor's Church on Church Point. The inn, being situated in a steep, narrow street leading down towards the sea, it was not until I was almost upon the harbour that I had my first real sight of the Cove. Morwella was a place very much larger than I would have expected of a fishing village. The reason lay immediately to the east of Church Point, itself easily distinguished by its square towered church. Starkly white against their dark surroundings and gouged out of the hillside, were the workings of a china clay quarry. A small railway carried pony-drawn trucks across the point and down to a harbour which served not only fishing boats, but small cargo vessels used to transport the clay – I supposed to some port and thence by barge to the vicinity of the midland pottery towns.

But none of this was enough to divert my attention from what lay at the western end of Morwella Cove. Pierce had described his home as "isolated, gloomy, even frightening". I now had little doubt that I was looking at it, albeit from some distance off.

The cove itself was a sweeping curve, perhaps all of a mile in length. Its eastern boundary was marked by Church Point with the harbour and village clustered closely about it. Its western extremity ended in a much longer promontory, the sea having broken through it towards its landward end, leaving nothing at that point but a narrow bridge of rock. Further towards the land, but still upon the promontory, was a house. Its jumbled lines of roofs and chimneys were features which, in so many houses, give a sense of charm. Yet, unaccountably, this house had about it a curiously unwelcoming appearance. The fanciful might well have described it as one of "silent, brooding menace"! Perhaps it was no more than a preconception which Pierce's description had put into my mind. But that could not account for my having much those same feelings about the one feature which I have yet to describe.

On the seaward end of the promontory – in truth an island but for its rock bridge – five huge stones, none less than several feet in height, and of considerable breadth, were so arranged that they had the appearance of the fingers of a giant hand. I supposed them to be both ancient and man made, though I had never seen anything of quite their like before.

....

"Your observation, Dr Watson, is astonishingly accurate. The stones are, in fact, known locally as the *Giant's Fingers*. In more scientific terms, they undoubtedly are the remains of some ancient henge – a huge double circle of stones, of which all but those five have long been claimed by the sea."

My informant, the Revd Matthew Laycock, rector of St Mor's Church, I had found with Holmes in the churchyard. They were discussing the very thing which had so captured my imagination when I had first seen it from above the harbour.

"I have been explaining to Mr Holmes," Mr Laycock continued, "that I am no expert upon these matters. Such knowledge as I have, you might say has been thrust upon me by an unfortunate combination of circumstances."

Mr Laycock was obviously a quite young man – tall, athletic in build, with a boyish face and an unruly shock of red hair which gave him a most unclerical appearance. His predecessor, Dr Samuel Lyte, had been both historian and archaeologist, and a frequent contributor upon those subjects to the pages of both learned, and, occasionally, more popular journals.

"Though Dr Lyte departed from this world some four years ago, his writings continue to bring a steady trickle of visitors – both those of more serious mind, usually desirous of examining the Morwella Stones, and the idly curious, whose interest is more likely to centre upon 'Black Jack Darke', one time squire, parson, magistrate, smuggler, and murderer of this parish! Since neither category of visitor is ever entirely successful in accomplishing their mission, they seem, invariably, to feel that I can be of next best assistance to them!"

The explanation of Mr Laycock's seemingly curious statement, lay in the house which I had already taken to be the home of Nathan Pierce. It had been built in the last century by John Darke, whose qualifications Mr Laycock had just listed. The combination of squire, parson and magistrate was not then uncommon, though less commonly accompanied by that of smuggler and murderer! It was for the purpose of smuggling that the house had been sited in that position.

"Though I would not vouch for it," Mr Laycock told us, "the house is said to contain secret passages which lead down to some of the several caves which can only be entered by boat at low tide. The promontory itself is quite unscalable. The only access to the house is therefore from the land, and that is not easily possible because of a high wall and iron gates. You can well imagine that the place is also rich in ancient, and somewhat frightening legend. And where all that did not serve to discourage unwelcome visitors, John Darke was said to have used more final solutions! It was on such evidence, as well as his smuggling, that he was eventually found guilty and hanged at Falmouth in 1786.

"I'm afraid, that since Darke House was bought by a Mr Pierce about three years ago, he has once more made full use of its impregnable situation to exclude all visitors. Not, I would hasten to add, for the same reasons or by the same methods as Black Jack Darke! He is merely a man who likes his privacy, but you will now understand why it is I who receive so many of his unwelcome and disappointed callers."

Whilst Mr Laycock felt that he had, by now, become well able to satisfy those wishful only to hear more of Black Jack Darke, he did not have the confidence to deal with those, "especially with the academics", who sought to be informed upon the Morwella Stones.

"I suppose that I must think myself fortunate that Dr Lyte did leave behind him a number of his notes and sketches, which I have set out in one room of the rectory where they may be inspected and copied. If you gentlemen would care to return there with me now, I will be pleased to show it to you. Perhaps I might also persuade you to purchase a small souvenir of your visit. I do have some photographs, which I sell, the proceeds being for the upkeep of the church."

"You are a photographer?" Holmes asked.

Inscribed on back – Morwella Stones, J. Tregennis, June 1889.

"No, Mr Holmes. But Morwella Cove does boast one other unexpected feature – a London photographer of very considerable skills. He has a studio in Clay Lane. And I'm told he has the other unusual qualification of being one of the few local people ever to be invited by Mr Pierce to Darke House."

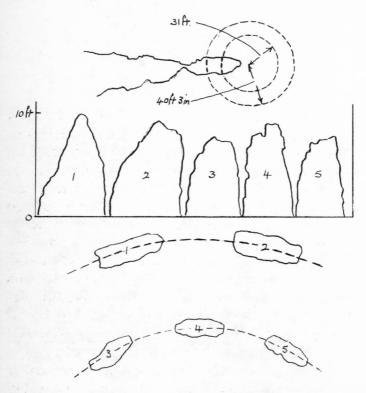

Assumed to be a tracing made by Watson or Holmes during their visit to the exhibition of Dr Lyte's papers.

Chapter Four

A Chapter of Surprises

We returned to the Fisherman's Rest for lunch. I had rarely known Holmes to take any deep interest in food. His diet was generally sparse and he often neglected to eat at all, if he saw it as occupying time which could be better spent in other pursuits. He failed even to react to the dish which the landlord brought to our table with what seemed considerable if unjustifiable pride! He informed us that it was a local dish with a name which sounded like "Stargazey Pie". Its contents did not require explanation, being readily deduced from the fish heads which stuck out through its crust – and which severally regarded one with malevolently glazed expressions!

Holmes made no comment on it, launching instantly into an account of his morning's work. Of the pie, I can only say that centring my mind fully upon what Holmes was saying, I found to be a most useful means of distracting my attention from what was on my plate!

That morning, having satisfied himself with his usual breakfast of coffee and toast, Holmes had first returned to the station at Morwella Halt to enquire which staff had been on duty in the last two days. It had then taken a visit to a cottage in the village to establish what I found to be a most surprising fact.

Pierce and his ward had arrived at Morwella Halt two nights ago, at precisely the time that one would have expected them, had they been on the 11.46 from Paddington. Holmes had also thought to ask the porter whom he had visited, whether he could remember how the girl was dressed. The man could not. It was dark and the station platform not well lit. It might have been a dark coloured mantle with a hood.

"But," I said, "we know that they were not on that train. I'm certain that we could not possibly have failed to see them if they had been."

"They were not on the train Watson, at least not until it had reached Exeter. Quite clearly, the train they caught in London was the 12.05 from Waterloo. Since the Paddington train takes the much longer route through Bristol to Exeter, the Waterloo train reaches Exeter first. It was then only necessary to change trains."

"Then Pierce did lie!" I said.

"No, Watson. He didn't. As I recall his words, he said that, 'at around midday, we should be on the train returning to Cornwall'. It was we who assumed that because he was staying at the Great Western, the train to which he referred was the 11.46 leaving from Paddington."

I didn't know what to make of that information. It did sound odd yet once more it seemed that Pierce was telling the truth. Holmes himself didn't seem willing to venture any opinion on his discovery, but perhaps I *was* beginning to see what Holmes had meant when he talked about every question having two possible answers. One of those questions was why Pierce had left the watch. Holmes had insisted that it was our invitation to Morwella Cove. I asked him when he intended to use it.

"It's done," he told me. "Just before I went to Church Point, I dispatched a note and the watch to Darke House. My messenger was our landlord's son – and I would have expected him to be back by now."

I asked what was in the note.

"I told Pierce that we had planned to spend some days on holiday in Cornwall and that since we had made no firm decisions as to our itinerary, we had thought to stop at Morwella Cove. I added that we found the place to be pleasant and that we might well remain here for a few days."

I said that if I were Pierce, I might not find that explanation very convincing. Holmes suggested that I reserve my judgement upon that until he had received a reply which, if he was not mistaken, was about to reach us!

A presentable youth of perhaps fifteen years had appeared at our table, breathlessly brandishing a letter. He was anxious to explain the causes of his lateness. The gates of Darke House had been locked. There was a bell, which he assumed could be heard from the house, but it had taken some long time before anyone had answered it. A woman had come to the gates. She had taken the note and the watch, but not unlocked the gates – telling the youth to wait outside. After what had seemed an even longer time, she had returned with the letter he now carried.

Holmes opened the letter, glancing briefly at its contents before passing it to me.

Dear Mr Holmes

What an amazing coincidence that it had already been your intention to visit Cornwall, and how very kind of you to use that circumstance to return the watch, which was my brother's, and is of great sentimental value to me. I do dearly wish that I could express my gratitude in some more suitable form than this brief note, but I have been overtaken by events which make that utterly impossible.

My worst fears have been realised. Not only have all of Emily's imaginings returned, but her behaviour has become so wildly unpredictable, even violent, that I have come to fear for her safety. I have had no alternative but to send away all of my staff, save one – a woman whose discretion I can trust and who has some experi-

ence in nursing.

You may think me foolish, Mr Holmes, but still I cling to the hope that Emily's cure might be but two days off – the day of her twenty-first birthday. I am finding it increasingly hard to believe that it will be so, but time will soon prove me right or wrong.

I note your intention to remain in Morwella for a few days. If the miracle, for which I most fervently pray, does occur, then it would give me good cause for celebration. It would be such a pleasure and privilege if both you and Dr Watson were able to join me in it.

I returned the letter to Holmes. "That is one invitation," I said, "that you may be sure we shall not be receiving. From Pierce's description of his ward's mental condition, he *does* need a miracle to cure her. A twenty-first birthday will certainly not do it!"

Holmes was looking intently at the head of a herring which stared back at him from his plate.

"Of course," he said, "I do respect your medical opinion, Watson. As to miracles, as Mr Pierce rightly observes, time will tell. But since *we* may have none of it to waste, and if you have now finished your lunch, we have a call to make – in Clay Lane."

The shop and studio of J. Tregennis, "Photographic Artist", were located in an ordinary house. The window-sill within one of the ground floor windows had been extended to provide a small area for display. Upon this occasion, it contained a single item, tastefully framed, and set upon a miniature easel. I say "item", because it was a matter of some doubt as to whether it was in fact a photograph or a painting. What seemed in no doubt, was the subject. It was Emily Pierce!

"You are certain of that, Watson?" Holmes asked.

I was.

"I know that we didn't see the girl in Baker Street for very long, but I'm certain of the blonde hair and blue eyes – and one thing that you can't mistake is the blue dress and the hat with the ostrich feathers. I'm not expert in such matters, but I would imagine that there isn't another dress and hat exactly like them. I must say that he's got the colour perfect."

Holmes decided that we should go in. The door bell had not ceased tinkling on its spring before a curtain was pulled back from across an arched doorway, and a man entered the small shop. He was tall, quite stooped and wearing thick lensed spectacles, though his age was probably younger than first appearances suggested.

"Ah!" he said, "you are about to tell me that you have not come in to buy. You are certainly not amateur photographers, who are usually so slung about with leather and canvas bags and tripods, that they have difficulty even in entering the premises. You are much too casually dressed to have come to have your own photographs taken, and the only other commissions I would normally get in this shop are for infants, weddings, tombstones and fishing boats. You don't look as though you would fall into any of those categories. Therefore, you are either seeking directions – or you are interested in what I have in the window. I would guess, the latter."

I looked at Holmes. His face showed nothing of the amusement that I was experiencing at that moment and I was waiting only to see whether Holmes was now about to outdo him with a still more devastating exhibition of deductive reasoning. I was disappointed.

"Astonishing!" was his first comment. "And you are completely correct in your assumption. We were doing no more than explore the village, when we came upon your studio – and that remarkable portrait in your window. We should be greatly obliged to you if you would settle an argument between us as to whether it is a coloured photograph or a painting."

"It's both," was the answer. "In the trade, we call it an 'oleograph' – an oil painting which is done over a photographic print. I don't think you'll see many of them outside of London. Expensive you see, and not much demand, not in a small place like Morwella Cove."

"A great shame that your obvious talent is wasted then," Holmes observed.

"Oh! No sir," Tregennis informed us. "You see I did work for a studio in London, but I have an ageing parent." He pointed to the ceiling – I assumed to indicate that the ageing parent was lodged in the room above us. "No way would my mother live in London so, being as you might say a case of Mahomet and the mountain – here I am! It's a very poor living I'd make here, but for the London studio still sending me work – more sometimes than I'd like."

"So the young woman in the window isn't local?"

"It happens, sir, that she is – a Miss Pierce. Mr Pierce, he owns that house all on its own, beside those big stones that you must have noticed at the west end of the cove." Holmes nodded assent. "What's in the window's a twenty-first birthday present. Of course, the young lady knows I went to the house a month since, to take her photograph, but the painting's a surprise. Mr Pierce did take it away when it was finished, but then he brought it back again a few days later. He was afraid that Miss Pierce might find it in the house, and spoil the surprise. So he suggested I keep it here till the birthday. He thought I might like to put it in the window – Miss Pierce not being one for coming into the village so not likely to see it."

Holmes thanked him for his kindness in settling our argument, and for the interesting conversation. We were about to leave, with Tregennis accompanying us to the shop door when, suddenly, he peered hard at our faces through his thick spectacles.

"Pardon my rudeness, gentlemen, but do you by any chance see the *Strand Magazine*?"

"No," Holmes told him, "though I'm sure I've heard of it."

"I ask," he said, "because you gentlemen do bear a striking resemblance to Mr Sherlock Holmes, the famous London detective, and his assistant Dr Watson. Their cases are published regularly, with illustrations, in the *Strand*. I'm a great follower, you see, of Mr Sherlock Holmes' cases – and his methods. You might have noticed my little demonstration of his methods of deduction when you entered the shop."

"Indeed, I did, Mr Tregennis!" Holmes told him, with feigned admiration. "I see that Mr Brown and I must buy a copy of this *Strand Magazine* and take a look at our famous likenesses. I suppose that we will not obtain a copy in Morwella."

Tregennis confirmed that we would not. He would have been happy to show us one of his own copies, but for the fact that they were temporarily stored in a cupboard in his mother's room and at this time of day she would be taking her afternoon rest. But if we would care to call back at some other time . . . Holmes told him that might not be possible since we did not expect to be staying long in Morwella.

"I'm afraid," Tregennis added, by way of parting comment, "that in a village like this there is not a great deal of interest in crime and detection –

indeed none, except for myself, and Mr Pierce."

In the short time that we had been in the shop, it had begun to rain, quite heavily and, to judge from the dark cloud blowing up from the east, the rain looked likely to continue for some hours. Holmes had turned up the collar of his coat. There wasn't even a flicker of a smile on his face when he said, "Come on, Mr Brown. Since I deduce that we are about to get very wet, I suggest that we return to the inn."

nothing has happened to change my mind! My visit to Forbes convinced me that Pierce was not only telling the truth, but that he had no designs on his ward's inheritance. He could so easily have had her committed to an institution.

Their taking the train from Waterloo and not Paddington looks odd. It could have something to do with Holmes frightening the girl when we chased her cab – or perhaps Pierce had some business to transact late that morning – at a place nearer to Waterloo than Paddington.

Pierce's house is just as he described it – and his sending the servants away is what I'd expect after what he said to us at Baker Street. I'm sure he's wrong in imagining that Emily will be cured after her birthday – but you can't blame the man for hoping!

Tregennis was a bit of a surprise! But
if we learned anything there, it was
only more proof of Pierce's innocence
of any criminal intention. You don't
have an expensive portrait done of
someone that you are planning to
murder!

It was interesting to learn that
Pierce was interested in crime — but
perhaps not altogether surprising. He
had himself admitted (at Baker Street)
to knowing of Holmes — he said he'd
mentioned the name to Emily.

STILL HAVEN'T ASKED HOLMES ABOUT
THE DOG!

Chapter Five

A Time of Decision

The rain which had driven us back to the inn, continued and, as the afternoon wore on, the wind steadily increased to a howling gale. Certain that we'd not be leaving the inn again that day, I went upstairs to my room to fetch the reading matter which I usually carried in my luggage for just such occasions. Though I'd felt in no state that morning to do more than glance at the view from my window, I now discovered that I could actually see the Morwella Stones through a gap in the roofs of the buildings opposite. It was a discovery of no very special interest, except that the wind's fury was now such that, even in the failing light, I could see the spray from the waves actually breaking over the stones themselves. I had judged them to be some thirty feet above even the high tide!

Thankfully, the evening meal was a very acceptable one of roast beef and, following it, we repaired to the bar room where, considering the dreadful state of the weather, we found it to be surprisingly well filled with local residents. Holmes, never neglectful of any opportunity, contrived to fall into conversation with a group of fishermen, and very soon had turned the subject from herring to Darke House! In view of Pierce's reputation as something of a recluse, I did not expect that Holmes would learn very much – except perhaps for the kind of wild rumour which always grows around situations where little or nothing is known with any certainty. We were regaled with several tales of Black Jack Darke, but of Pierce himself, we learned nothing new except that none of his servants was local and that they were positively discouraged from coming into the village. The tale had spread that most of them had very recently left the house but, since they had also left the district, no-one was even guessing at the reasons.

The bar room fire, the lack of a night's sleep on our journey down, and perhaps too much of the strong local ale, soon had me nodding off to sleep, though it was not yet ten o'clock. I excused myself and went to my room. I had not counted on the coldness of the room or the noise of the wind and rain. I had often found that sitting in bed and composing my notes on the day's events was a sure recipe for bringing on sleep, but I had heard the clock on the staircase strike twelve before the recipe must finally have succeeded.

The next morning was calm and bright, though still cold. I found Holmes at breakfast – looking very fresh and, I thought, unusually cheerful for that time of morning. I asked what plans he had for the day.

"None," was his answer, "except to keep ourselves readily available at all times."

My natural question was to ask, "Available for what?"

"An invitation to Darke House, Watson. What else?"

The events of yesterday had done nothing but strengthen my own conviction that, for once, Holmes was wrong. I was sure that there would be no invitation – but what Holmes had said still left me curious to know why he should imagine that *if* an invitation were to come, it could be today. Pierce's letter had stated very clearly that it was not even possible until after Emily Pierce's twenty-first birthday. And that meant in two days' time, at the soonest.

"No, Watson. I agree with what you said yesterday. If Emily Pierce's mental condition is as you suppose, it will not be cured by a birthday and, therefore, there will be no invitation – not, that is, to ask us to join in some celebration.

"The invitation which I had in mind would be for a very different purpose. I am not certain of the timing, except that it must be either today or tomorrow. My concern is not to miss the opportunity when, or as you would say Watson 'if', it comes. But I am not suggesting that we need spend all of our day in the inn. It is a fine morning, and I learned from last night's conversation that the fishing boats should just now be arriving back in the cove. Perhaps we might visit the harbour."

I noticed that Holmes gave careful instruction to the landlord as to where we might be found, should any message arrive before we had returned to the inn.

Several boats were already in the harbour and unloading their catches ready for the fish auction that would take place later in the morning. Though herring and mackerel were the predominant fish, there were many other varieties including crabs and lobsters, these last very much alive and making a great clattering of claws in the bottom of some of the boats. A group of fishermen, some of whom I recognised from the night before, were standing on the quayside, and engaged in what sounded like some loud, if not too serious, banter.

"I keeps telling you, George, don't I, that you're a courtin' trouble puttin' your pots there. 'Tis the spirits of the *Morwella Stones* givin' you a warnin'."

"Then 'tis a funny thing, Tom Burke, that they be a choosin' for to do it. My missus has one just like it – and that she uses for boilin' puddins!"

"I does beg your pardon, George! You wasn't tellin' me it was one o' your Annie's puddins.

And here's me thinkin' it were a stone. 'Tis no small wonder you suffers so chronic with your belly!"

I'm sure the exchange would have gone on, had "George" not noticed Holmes and myself approaching.

"Now here's two educated city gentlemen who's not as daft as you, Tom Burke, and who'll maybe be givin' us a sensible answer."

The group parted so that we could now see the subject of discussion. George lifted a crab pot from the quay so that we might see it more closely. In the opening was a white cotton bag, partly closed at the neck by a drawstring. Something was clearly holding the bag firmly in place in the pot.

"'Tis a stone in the bag," George said, "a sight bigger than the hole in the pot and no way of shiftin' it. Question is, if 'er won't come out, how did 'er get in in the first place!"

Holmes asked for the pot to be held upside down. Having loosened the string he put his hand into the bag so he could feel the shape of the stone. "When I tell you, Watson, pull the bag down." He seemed to give the stone a sharp twist – shouting, "Pull" at the same time as he started to withdraw his hand. The bag and stone came free – to the accompaniment of an admiring cheer.

"You now see, gentlemen, how it got in. By sheer chance, it landed on the pot at the one quite critical angle which made its entry possible. Can

I ask where the pot would have been when it happened?"

"In a good fifteen feet of water," George answered him, "– just yon far side of Morwella Point."

"How close to the cliff?" Holmes asked.

"Maybe twenty-five, thirty feet. You can't get no closer nor that for the rocks."

"Then we know 'how' and 'where'," Holmes observed. "I find 'why' to be the most interesting question, but the answer to that might take me a little time. Perhaps if I might borrow the bag?"

He was told to keep it. It was small enough reward for not having to cut the pot open to get it out.

....

The bag was wet and, having been in the boat, smelled of fish. Holmes suggested that this might best be remedied by carrying it around for a while in the morning's cold but freshening breeze. We watched the rest of the boats return, then walked to a large shed at the back of the harbour where the fish auction took place. By the time the last box had been sold, and the earlier sales, already stacked on carts, were on their way to the station, it was almost time for lunch.

No message for Holmes had been left at the inn. After a good night's sleep and a morning in the sea air, I had developed a healthy appetite. I was pleased to be able to satisfy it with nothing more unusual than a good mutton stew. The dining room began to darken quite noticeably as we ate our meal, and I feared that we might be about to have a storm like that of the previous day. In that, I was wrong, but a steady drizzle of rain had begun and, when I went once more to my room to collect the same reading matter which had served me so well on the afternoon before, the Morwella Stones were completely hidden by a wet sea mist.

Having settled myself opposite to Holmes in front of a well-tended bar-room fire I was unprepared for the appearance of either the inn's kitchen maid, or what she handed to Holmes. It looked like the bag we had obtained that morning, but it appeared to have been freshly laundered!

"It still smelled of fish," was Holmes' explanation, which I accepted, though I did think that ironing it seemed a little unnecessary! "Now, Watson," Holmes continued. "We know where this ended up. You must have formed an opinion as to where it came from."

I had. It could only have been tossed from the top of the cliff on which the Stones stood.

"Good! Now tell me why."

"The bag must have contained something, apart from the stone. That was only to make it sink. Whatever else was in the bag must have fallen out."

"I think not, Watson. When I first examined the bag, I *could* see into it, but I had to untie the drawstring before I could get my hand inside. The fishermen might have untied it, but wouldn't have retied it. When the bag was thrown from the cliff, it contained nothing but a stone. I can only suppose –"

Holmes stopped in mid sentence. Our landlord had come into the room, with a woman. She was completely wrapped about in a heavy, dark mantle and hood. She was small, and looked wet, but I could tell little more about her. The landlord pointed towards the fire where Holmes and I were seated, then left the room as the woman came towards us – the hood slipping from her head as she walked. Her face was narrow, with high cheek bones. The lips were thin and the dark eyes slightly bulging – to a degree which suggested that she was myopic. The hair was black, greying above the temples and held tight back in a bun. I found the woman's appearance rather forbidding. I assumed that she brought the message which Holmes had so clearly expected, and looked across the fire towards him. I'd just time to realise that the bag, which a moment ago he'd been holding in his hands, was suddenly no longer visible, before the woman spoke.

"Are you Dr Watson?"

Because I'd assumed it was Holmes she sought, the question startled me. With some hesitation, I replied that I was. She handed me a letter which I opened and read. It *was* from Pierce.

"Listen to this, Holmes! 'The bearer of this letter is Miss Fordyce, the one remaining member of my staff of whom I spoke in my note to Mr Holmes. I am sure that Mr Holmes will have made you aware of my present circumstances. It may not, therefore, come as a complete surprise to you when I say that I find myself in most desperate need of medical help. There is a man in the village, but I have good reason not to have to call upon his services. I know that I presume upon an all too short acquaintance, but I pray that you will not refuse my plea for help.' It's signed by Pierce."

I turned to the woman.

"As a doctor," I said, "I'm not likely to refuse such a request, but perhaps, Miss Fordyce, you can tell me something more of the nature of this emergency."

"It's Miss Emily," she replied. "More than that, I don't think Mr Pierce would want me to say. I have a horse and trap outside."

I told her I'd prefer that Holmes came with us.

"I think that Mr Pierce was assuming that Mr Holmes would wish to come with you, Dr Watson. He did tell me to be sure to take the trap that carries three."

....

In the poor light and continuing drizzle, and now at close quarters, Darke House looked infinitely more gloomy and unwelcoming than I could ever have imagined, even from my first impressions of it. As the trap drew up at its main entrance, the door was opened by Pierce himself. Holmes and I dismounted. Miss Fordyce drove on – I assumed to lodge the horse and trap in the coachhouse and stables. Pierce had come down the steps to meet us.

"You don't know how grateful I am to see you, Dr Watson and, of course, you Mr Holmes. But this is not the place to be making explanations. Let us go into the house."

As could have been expected, the inside of the house was still darker than it was outside. Holding an oil lamp to light our way, Pierce led us down a winding corridor and into a large, well-furnished and most unusually well-lit room, where a blazing fire also added to its unexpectedly cheerful atmosphere.

"Let me take your coats. I should have done so before. You will see I am unused to the absence of my servants."

He laid the coats on a chair.

"Miss Fordyce will take them when she returns. Emily is upstairs, locked in her room. I will take you to her in a moment, Dr Watson, but let me first prepare you for what you will find. I spoke in my note to you, Mr Holmes, of Emily becoming violent. I fear that since I wrote it, her condition has become steadily worse. I have given her quite large doses of tincture of opium but, it seems, to little effect. Miss Fordyce has seen more of her than I and may tell you more. She should be with us in a moment."

Pierce crossed to one of the large windows to pull the curtains together but stopped, his attention obviously caught by something outside the window.

"It's Emily!" was all he said, as he began to run towards the door of the room. Holmes and I rushed to the window. We could see the figure of a woman, bare footed and dressed, it seemed, only in a nightgown. With her long, blonde hair streaming out in the wind, she was running away from the house and towards the seaward end of the promontory. Already she had reached the narrow bridge of rock, beyond which the Morwella Stones were just visible through the mist and rain.

Pierce had gone. Holmes now followed and I came last, blundering back along the dark corridor. When I reached the main door, I could no longer see the girl. Pierce was at the bridge, and Holmes only yards behind him. In a moment, both were gone from sight. I was not to see them again until I had myself reached the farther side of the Stones. Of the girl, I could still see nothing. Already I was fearing the worst, when I heard hysterical cries – from somewhere behind me!

I turned and ran back between the Stones. Miss Fordyce was standing on the bridge – still dressed in the mantle she had worn when she had come to the inn. Her neatly drawn back hair had come partly loose and hung, lank and wet, over her face. Blood was running down one of her cheeks. Perhaps because of the sight of me, her cries had subsided. She now stood silent, a pitiful sight as tears welled from the dark eyes, to mingle with the rain and blood which streaked the face and dripped from the long wet wisps of black hair.

Pierce and Holmes were suddenly beside me. Seeing Pierce, the woman stepped towards him. "I couldn't stop her, sir! I'd only gone upstairs to take off my wet clothes, when Miss Emily called out to me. She sounded so calm that I unlocked her door. And then she attacked me! I wasn't expecting it. I think I fell. Perhaps I hit my head. I know that when I got up, she was gone. I saw the front door was open and . . . Is she . . . ?"

Pierce said nothing, but stepped forward and put his arm about the woman's shoulders. "You must not blame yourself, Miss Fordyce." He turned back towards me. "I will take her back to the house. Mr Holmes will show you what we have found. I'm afraid, Dr Watson, that there is nothing that you can do for Emily now."

I followed Holmes back between the Stones. He stopped almost at the end of the promontory. "Take care, Watson. You need to be close to the edge – and the grass is slippery." Perhaps ten feet down, caught on a projection of rock, was a piece of torn white cloth. Below it there was nothing but twenty feet of cliff face – rising sheer out of a black, heaving, foam-flecked cauldron of boiling sea.

Holmes had surely been wrong in supposing there was any mystery here. There was only tragedy. I found myself wishing that he'd been right. Perhaps, I told him – if he had been right, it might have ended in some other, less tragic way.

"But it is not 'ended', Watson. Nathan Pierce knew exactly how to rouse my curiosity and suspicions – in a manner which would in no way threaten his fiendishly brilliant plan, but would surely bring me here at this precise moment to bear witness to the success of it!"

"But I brought you here!" I said. "Pierce sent for me, and it was I who suggested that you came with me."

"Pierce knew that I would insist upon coming with you. Be assured, Watson, that had I come to Morwella alone, he'd have found some other reason to bring me here. But there are more urgent matters. Emily Pierce is alive. She has not committed suicide, but she is about to be murdered!"

"By Pierce?"

"Who else, Watson?"

"But no murderer invites an audience to witness the deed!"

"You don't understand, Watson, and there is little time to explain. Pierce cannot know that I suspect murder, though you may be certain that the possibility has not escaped him. But it makes no difference to his plans. He is supremely confident that whatever my suspicions, I can do nothing to change those plans – because he is sure that I do not have one single shred of proof. This far, Watson, he has judged me well, but perhaps not well enough. I do have no proof, but I do still have one weapon – bluff. And there, my friend, lies my dilemma. If I use that weapon, then I might yet save the girl's life. If I use it and fail, then I could well have two deaths on my conscience!"

I understood nothing of what Holmes had said, but my instinct was to offer any help that I could.

"The decision must be mine, Watson, but there is a way in which you might possibly help. Go back to the house. Use whatever means you can to ensure that neither Pierce nor Miss Fordyce attempt to return here before I can, myself, come back. You have your medical bag with you?"

"Yes."

"Have you a styptic pencil in it?"

"To stop bleeding – yes, I have, but . . ."

"Please, no more questions, Watson – and give me the scarf that you still have around your neck."

I had neglected to remove my scarf when I had taken off my coat. It was wet, but I gave it to Holmes.

"Now go, Watson, back to the house, and quickly!"

Chapter Six

A Battle of Minds

I found Pierce in the room to which he'd taken us when we'd first arrived. He was alone. I asked what had happened to Miss Fordyce. He surprised me by telling me that she was on her way to the village to seek help.

"– though I can't imagine what help she thinks is possible. There can be no doubt of what's happened. Once across the stone bridge, there's nowhere anyone could remain hidden. It's impossible that Emily could have left that part of the promontory. I was the first to follow her, then Mr Holmes, then yourself Dr Watson – and then Miss Fordyce. Emily couldn't have recrossed the bridge without being seen. And I assume that you have now seen what can only be a part of her nightgown. Emily couldn't, of course, swim – but no-one could fall into that sea and survive."

I expressed my surprise that Miss Fordyce had

felt well enough to leave for the village so quickly – though I did appreciate that it would be necessary at least to inform the police.

"The haste wasn't mine, Dr Watson. The blood on her face from the attack Emily made on her was from no more than scratches. At the same time, she was very obviously shaken and distressed. I did my best to persuade her to give herself time to recover. But it was she who insisted on leaving. I think that she had some terrible feeling of guilt about being responsible for what had happened, though you heard me try to reassure her. I could see that she desperately wanted to do something to help. I thought it perhaps best, in the circumstances, not to attempt to prevent her." He paused. "Mr Holmes is not with you."

I was saved from having to invent an explanation. Holmes had just entered the room. His first question was to ask the whereabouts of Miss Fordyce. I said she had gone to the village. If Holmes' face showed any of the surprise which I'd felt on hearing that news – I missed it. My attention was centred upon the piece of white cotton which Holmes was holding in his hand.

"Is that . . .? But it was ten feet down the cliff and impossible to . . ."

"Impossible to climb down – yes, Watson – but not impossible to retrieve the cloth with the aid of a pencil, knotted into the end of your scarf, though I'm afraid I've lost your scarf. I'll buy you another."

Pierce had stepped forward.

"I'm sure that it wasn't necessary for you to take the trouble, Mr Holmes, but I suppose that the police will regard it as useful evidence."

He held out his hand to take the cloth.

"A moment, Mr Pierce – if you would just indulge me in a small experiment. Watson, you will have a styptic pencil in your medical bag. If I might borrow it?"

I gave Holmes the pencil. Pierce watched in silence as Holmes drew it several times across the cloth. "It will take a little time. I don't know the extent of your knowledge of chemistry, Mr Pierce, but I should perhaps explain that a styptic pencil is made by melting nitrate of silver and casting it into sticks." He was looking at the cloth, on which purplish streaks had begun to appear. "Other than its use for stopping bleeding – I'm sure you use one in shaving – it also reacts with common salt to form the chloride of silver. That is a white substance, but one which breaks down in the light to form metallic silver – and is the basis of photography. The dark marks you can now see on the cloth mean that the cloth is soaked in salt water."

"I'm sorry Mr Holmes. I'm sure that is most interesting, but I feel that it is not a moment for you to be giving chemistry lessons. Perhaps you are forgetting the very sad and tragic nature of the circumstances which bring us here."

"I am forgetting nothing," was Holmes' sharp retort. "You say that this is a piece torn from your ward's nightgown as she fell from the cliff. If it is, then it was hanging there for no more than a few minutes. Yet it is soaked in salt water – sea spray. I see only one explanation – that the cloth had been hanging in that position, probably for several hours."

It was some moments before Pierce answered.

"If that were so, Mr Holmes, then I see the reason for your puzzlement, though not the reason for your obvious suspicions in the first place. There is a much simpler explanation. Emily fell before she reached the edge. Yesterday, the whole promontory was covered in sea spray. The grass must be soaked in salt water."

If this was Holmes' bluff, it had failed! Yet his face showed no trace of concern as, for some reason, he put his hand round to his back – inside his jacket.

"That is certainly an alternative explanation but, because of our shared interest in crime, I need hardly tell you, Mr Pierce, that the final interpretation of evidence rarely rests upon a single clue."

As he finished the sentence, Holmes withdrew his hand from behind his back. He was now holding a white, drawstring bag, bulging with whatever filled it. He tossed it onto the carpet where it landed with a thud.

"I have no need to open it, Mr Pierce – since you know its contents – apart from a stone – a nightgown and a blonde wig. I'm afraid that Miss

Fordyce – in her haste – and perhaps because of her rather obvious shortsightedness, failed to notice that the bag had not left the cliff, but was caught by its drawstring just inches below the edge."

Pierce was now visibly disturbed. Holmes instantly pressed home his advantage.

"What more do I have to do? – Have you detained until I can confront you with the woman who copied the dress and hat from the painting that Tregennis did for you? Do I also have to produce the girl who wore those copies when she visited Baker Street – the same girl whom you had earlier taken to visit Forbes – the girl whom you employed to impersonate your ward? You are going to be arrested, Pierce. But I think it is still within your power to determine upon what charge – 'murder', for which you will most surely hang, or 'attempted murder', for which a good lawyer might get you a shorter prison sentence than you deserve!"

Pierce had moved to the fireplace. He grasped a part of the elaborate carving and twisted it. Nearby, an opening had appeared in the wall panelling behind a small table. He picked a lighted lamp from the table, at the same time, pushing the table to one side.

"Bring another lamp," he said. "It may still not be too late."

....

The opening in the panelling revealed a steep,

narrow, stone staircase, leading many feet down through the rock to one of the sea caves of which Mr Laycock had spoken. It was there that we found Emily Pierce, deeply drugged with opium and dressed only in a torn nightgown. The piece of cloth caught on the cliff would be later found to fit exactly with an area torn from the gown. In less than an hour, the girl would have been drowned by the rising tide and her body taken out to sea as the water later retreated. The body would not have shown the marks which might have been expected had it fallen thirty feet from the cliff. But the spot for the supposed fall had been carefully chosen. Beneath it, was a deep pool where the water would have stopped the movement of the falling body before it could touch the rocky bottom.

It took several hours for Emily Pierce to regain consciousness. She was later transferred to a private nursing home in St Austell, where she eventually made a full recovery. When Miss Fordyce had returned with the police, both she and Pierce were arrested.

Late that night, back in my room at the Fisherman's Rest, Holmes began with an apology for being right and an assurance that he had not brought me to Morwella Cove with a false promise that this might be the time when my instincts should prove better than his logic. "I have truly never been less certain," he confessed.

Holmes' suspicions had arisen, not for any

single reason so much as a coming together of events, events which had begun with the arrival of Nathan Pierce at Baker Street. Pierce claimed that his business was most urgent, yet he'd waited for several minutes in his cab before coming to the door. He gave as the reason for that urgency, that he believed it was the intention of his ward herself to visit Holmes that morning. But, if Emily Pierce did believe herself to be desperately in need of help, why had she not made Baker Street her first visit – and arrived as soon as Pierce?

Then came the watch. Why was Pierce carrying a second watch? Had he been at pains to draw attention to the fact? If he had left it deliberately, then for what purpose? If it was simply to supply a reason to get Holmes out of the house in an effort to return it, then there was no need for a second watch. Holmes was frankly puzzled, but decided to do the obvious. He *would* attempt to return the watch but, if Pierce *did* want him out of the house, then he'd no intention of missing what might occur during his supposed absence.

"But it was the girl, Watson, who really began to convince me that all might not be as it appeared. If I'd chosen to dress a woman in such a manner that her identity could not possibly be mistaken, even from a distance, I might have dressed her thus, but not on such a bitterly cold day! I'd not have expected even the most fashion conscious young woman to be so obviously ill clad. There certainly wasn't another to be seen in Baker Street that morning!

"What I was already suspecting then seemed to be confirmed by the unaccountably sudden manner of the girl's departure, as if she'd been warned of our presence. Nor could I believe it was coincidence that the driver of the girl's cab should subsequently prove to be among the most skilful and daring in London!"

Several things had now begun to fall into place in Holmes' mind. The appearance of a "distressed" girl at 221B, a girl fitting the description of Emily Pierce, at first appeared to confirm Pierce's story. Clearly, she could be seen. She could speak to Mrs Hudson, but *not* to Holmes. Pierce had offered an explanation for that, but there was another – that the girl was not the real Emily Pierce! And that would explain something else – why Pierce had waited for some time in the cab before coming to the house. He had seen my arrival. He knew that I was Watson – Holmes' friend.

"You see, Watson, Pierce had only allowed for two possibilities. Having found the watch, I would either leave the house in an attempt to return it or I would not. Your arrival produced a third possibility – that one of us would attempt to return the watch, while the other remained in the house. Pierce obviously needed time to consider whether his arrangements would also cover that new situation. We will never know what those arrangements were, but we must assume that

Pierce was satisfied that they were still adequate."

Unlike myself, Holmes had reached Paddington, not expecting to find either Pierce or his ward either at the hotel or the station. We neither of us then knew that Pierce, with the real Emily, would depart from Waterloo – nor, indeed, that if the girl in the cab had been the real Emily Pierce, she would have been going to the wrong station!

"I suppose," Holmes continued, "you might say that it was instinct more than logic that made me keep the watch. I had begun to think that I was being very cleverly manipulated by Nathan Pierce, but I didn't know for what purpose. And you, Watson, could see perfectly innocent explanations for everything – good enough, I might say, to make me doubt my own intuition. I think that if you had not brought me the information which you had obtained from your visit to Forbes, we might never have left London.

"Always the thought in my head had been that Pierce had designs upon his ward's inheritance. Further than that, I could not see – including whatever reason Pierce might have for wishing my involvement. I thought that you, perhaps, had told me! Pierce had made great play upon the 'disgrace' of admitting to there being any insanity in the family. But was the real reason that he couldn't have his ward committed to an institution, because the real Emily Pierce was not insane, and that the girl he'd taken to see Forbes, the same girl we saw in Baker Street, was *not* his ward? Forbes had conveniently warned of the danger of suicide. Was the real Emily Pierce going to be seen to commit suicide – and was I to be the principle witness! And even the watch had at last assumed a significance. I had been looking for a logical explanation. There was one, but it was the logic of illogicality! The second watch was not meant to make sense. Like so many other events which had occurred, its purpose was to puzzle and confuse – the surest way that Pierce could see of arousing my curiosity. I'm sure he intended me to think of using the watch as my invitation to Morwella Cove. Believe me, Watson, I still wasn't certain, not least because if I was being invited to witness murder, I couldn't begin to imagine how Pierce proposed to do it!"

Our arrival at Morwella Cove, and the first thirty-six hours that we had spent there, had served only to confirm my belief that Holmes was wrong – though Holmes had continued to see things quite differently. His discovery that Pierce and the real Emily Pierce had returned to Cornwall from Waterloo, fitted well with his theory. Knowing Holmes might go to Paddington with the watch, Pierce couldn't let him meet the real Emily. The news in Pierce's note that he'd sent the servants away, convinced Holmes that the scene was already being set for Emily Pierce's "suicide" – a "scene" offering everything from isolation and dangerous cliffs to sea caves and secret passages! Tregennis had revealed Pierce's interest in crime, and confirmed that Pierce probably had recognised me in Baker Street. He'd also answered the question of how Pierce had had one of Emily's most unusual and striking dresses copied for the false Emily to wear on her visit to 221B.

"And you, Watson, demonstrated the ease with which it is possible to make a false identification! You were certain the painting in Tregennis's window was of the same girl you saw in Baker Street – yet all you in fact remembered was a dress, a hat and blonde hair. You even mentioned her blue eyes, which you couldn't possibly have seen at that distance!"

Holmes did admit to one piece of sheer good fortune – the bag found in the crab pot by the fishermen. He now knew that one part of Pierce's plan required that something had to be disposed of – by throwing it in a weighted bag from the cliff into the sea.

....

The rest of the story can only be told with some considerable hindsight. When Pierce and the real Emily had returned from London to Darke House, Emily had promptly been drugged and confined to her room. Pierce had told the servants that she was suffering from some highly contagious disease and, for their own safety, he was sending them away until the crisis was over. Miss Fordyce, who had been only recently employed, but who had nursing experience, had "volun-

_d" to remain.

Emily was kept drugged and imprisoned. On the afternoon Miss Fordyce arrived at the inn, Emily was given a large dosage of opium and carried, unconscious, to the cave below the house. Having dropped Holmes and myself at the house Miss Fordyce drove the horse and trap to the coach house. There, she removed her outer clothing – including stockings and shoes, and put on a nightgown and a blonde wig. Pierce's arrival with the lamp in the room into which he took us, was Miss Fordyce's signal to start running towards the stone bridge. The unusually bright lighting of the room was to ensure that Holmes and I were effectively blinded to anything that we might have seen through the windows.

Several hours earlier, using a rope, Pierce had climbed down the cliff and secured the cloth torn from the nightgown in which the unconscious Emily would be dressed. Behind one of the Stones (marked '1' on the tracing of Dr Lyte's sketches), a bundle had been placed – consisting of a mantle and hood like that Miss Fordyce was wearing, a bag weighted with a stone, and a pair of elastic-sided boots. When Miss Fordyce reached the first of the Stones – and was hidden by it, she removed the wig and nightgown, placed them in the bag and threw it from the cliff. She then scratched her own face, slipped on the boots and covered her state of undress with the mantle. All this she did, even before Holmes had crossed the bridge. Hidden behind the outer edge of the stone, she waited until I also had passed, before returning to the bridge and beginning to shout.

"It was almost perfect," Holmes said. "The girl's body would have been eventually washed ashore – the piece missing from the nightgown matching that on the cliff. Forbes would not have seen the body, and would have no reason to suppose it was not the girl he had seen in London. He would have testified to the girl's state of mind and suicidal tendencies. Even if Emily's body had been found to contain unusually large quantities of opium, Forbes would also have testified that someone in that mental state, could be given such quantities without suffering unconsciousness."

"But it went wrong," I said. "You retrieved both the torn cloth and the bag."

"I did neither," Holmes replied. "The cloth, I tore from the back of my shirt and soaked it in the salty water on the grass. The bag was that found by the fishermen, and stuffed with your scarf, Watson. Pierce was sure he'd devised the perfect murder, so perfect, that he thought it deserved an audience. And what better audience than the 'famous Sherlock Holmes', who would then have to stand up in a coroner's court and give evidence which could support only one verdict – 'suicide'. He knew that even if I suspected murder, I had nothing to prove it. To Nathan Pierce, that would have been the ultimate accolade to his evil genius!"

..t you said that you could produce the
..man who copied the dress – and the girl who
came to Baker Street and who Pierce had taken to
see Forbes."

"Also bluff, Watson, and there lay the danger.
If Pierce had simply stood his ground I could have
done nothing. Emily Pierce would have died – but
I'd also have feared for another life – that of the
girl whom Pierce had hired to impersonate his
ward. There is no knowing what story he told her
in order to gain her services and little chance that
the girl would ever discover the true purpose for
which she'd been hired. Suppose there *was* a
paragraph in the London newspapers about
Emily Pierce's 'suicide'. Had the girl even read of
it, I imagine that she'd still have no reason to
suspect that she was an accomplice to murder!

"*But* Watson, what if my bluff had failed? Pierce
would have realised that I did not know the
whereabouts of the girl – but he *did*. He could
never have allowed me to find her, not alive!"

One question remained which Holmes could
not yet answer. "Who was Miss Fordyce, and
what was the reason for her involvement?" Part of
that answer, which only emerged during the
police investigation, couldn't have been more
unexpected. There *was* no inheritance!

Pierce was one of two trustees of Emily Pierce's
fortune. The other was a London lawyer called
Neville Fordyce. Following on the success of the
Suez Canal, they had invested Emily's money in

the Panama project – seeking to make a substantial profit for themselves. In 1889, the company went bankrupt amidst scandalous stories of mismanagement and corruption. Emily's money was all lost. Jane Fordyce was Neville's sister. She relied entirely upon her brother to keep her in a comfortable if not extravagant lifestyle. Her desire to retain that lifestyle required that she kept her brother out of gaol. The murder of Emily Pierce was a price which she was prepared to pay in order to do it.

....

Holmes had surely fulfilled one promise – to provide my mind with some distraction. But, in no way, could it compare with the joy I felt when, a few days later, I visited Holmes at Baker Street with the news that Mary was greatly improved, and coming home!

It was natural that on that occasion, Holmes and I should speak again of the dramatic events which we had so recently shared, nor was it surprising that I should recall a question which had slipped from my mind. "What had happened to Pierce's dog?"

"The servants took it with them," Holmes told me. "It would never have done to have it sniffing at mysterious bundles left behind stones, or secret panels in the walls! Which reminds me, Watson, that you still haven't told me how I knew Pierce had a dog."

I admitted to not knowing.

s boots, Watson – expensive, well-fitting,
ss boots, yet deeply creased across the uppers.
Well-fitting boots, not subject to heavy use,
should not crease in that way. Therefore, I supposed that Pierce had some reason to bend his feet
frequently – as one does if one flexes the knees
and feet in order to touch something near to the
ground. Since Pierce was already short, the most
obvious answer was a small dog."

I'd been looking at my own boots, observing
that I'd no dog, yet *my* boots were creased across
the uppers.

"I did say that Pierce's boots were well fitting,"
Holmes replied. "As to your boots, Watson, the
French have a phrase, 'à propos de bottes' –
meaning something of no real relevance!"

I thought it time to remind Holmes that he
owed me a new scarf.